BY THE SAME AUTHOR

A HIDDEN LANGUAGE

A HIDDEN LANGUAGE

MICHAEL CULLUP

Greenwich Exchange
London

Greenwich Exchange, London

First published in Great Britain in 2020
All rights reserved

Printed and bound by imprintdigital.com
Cover design by December Publications
Tel: 07951511275

Greenwich Exchange website: www.greenex.co.uk

Cataloguing in Publication Data is available from the British Library

Cover art: courtesy of Shutterstock

ISBN: 978-1-910996-33-1

for Jean

CONTENTS

1

A hand moves over the page.
A mass that concentrates.
A presence that watches,
writing.

Clouds pass from thought to thought
across a vacancy that space can only dream of,
timeless in their extinction.

I could disappear this minute
taking the world with me
into a darkness I wouldn't know was there.
But I hold on
as blood thickens in my neck.

2

The birds among the trees
open their beaks in silence.
I read the sounds
in a surge of silent wind.
Branches dance above me
in a blue sky.
The spongy grass yields to my pressing feet.
I settle where sounds have left the air
and reached the ground,
silent as moss.

3

Like a second skin
smothering the white
and bringing it to perfection,
the dazzle leans away from the wall
and dips to shadows.
There is a restlessness which itches for something new
and finds it in the grass
among weeds which are as fetching
as expensive flowers:
the common dandelion,
yellower than the sun that smiles today,
rich with defiance.
Among the grass, springing from a bed of leaves,
it waves its golden head.
Pluck it and it will bleed:
its blood whiter than any birch tree,
bitter as gall,
a threat of something restless, something ill.

4

More leaves fall from the lime.
Beyond the trim cypress
the eucalyptus sways,
shapeless, hanging out sideways.
The ivy on the wall keeps tight to the stone,
a flutter at the edges.

Rowan berries hang in bright orange clusters.
A desultory wind plays in the silver birch.
And there, beside the garage,
three chalk-white mushrooms.

The Bramley tree sags with the weight of cookers
and even the Crab is bitterly dense with fruit.
Hips, haws, blackberries, berries on cotoneaster,
firethorn, sloe,
everything swelling
and even the leanest creature fattening up.

The lime tree branches
shake in a sudden flurry
swept by a surge of wind.
The yellow leaves, tested beyond endurance,
let go and fall away.
They are blown into corners
or scattered on the grass
or pushed against the shed by the bullying wind

and one
caught on a tag of rose

could be a flag:
a sign of the year
beaten, stripped and plundered,
surrendering its tattered remnants to the winter.

Over it all
presiding like an ancient king
is the cankered apple, tortuously bent,
whose stretched extremities are breaking down,
littering bits;
whose empty trunk is flailed by the restless buddleia.

Where do we go when everything is finished?

5

The bird to his tree is called,
the snake to his stone,
and the waters plunder the soft enveloping moss.
Mountain ranges gather to the clouds
tumults of thunder.
The rising wind thrashes tormented trees.
Oceans of darkness, hidden by weeds,
stagnate.
Later, a single voice is heard
singing of lamentation.

6

Afternoons are so much shorter now
and the evenings come on so quickly.
After the dead fish, floating in with the tide,
the rock of the empty boat
and its rotting timbers.
After the heat of summer,
frost.
The ice lies inches thick on the flooded fens
but there are no skaters.
The ploughland, sick with acid,
lies under snow.
There are no birds.

7

It's dusk:
the dark is coming in
like a door closing slowly.
The light between the door and something else
is becoming something else:
becoming dark.

My neighbours hide behind their panel fences,
passers-by talk suddenly and are gone.
The darkness doesn't talk to me.
The light inside throws shadows on the lawn.
Life is so dark.
Outside, it thickens early,
reaches to the trees and climbs the branches.
The leaves are gathering its immensity.

After comes the wind,
searching odd corners
for somewhere to get in:
rattling of windows,
creaking on the stairs,
doors suddenly shutting with a bang
when there's no one there.
The television flickers their exchanges.
There is hardly room to speak amid such outrage.

In the gathering shadows
beasts move,
shaking from their hairy coats
a crust of autumn leaves.

Shambolic, heavy,
they lumber through the bushes.
They roar in the dark
and tear the fences down,
frightening the fox, who pricks up his ears and runs.
They are the scourge of order,
the suburban nightmare.
Open the door an inch
and you smell the scent
left on the patio broom.
The empty pots are staled with their heady urine.
Their stools litter the path.

8

Last night the lights went out
and all the world went dark.
Trees were enormous thicknesses all around me
and calls came from the depths of the dark forest.
A horse whinnied and shied away,
hooves plunging in the heavy mud.
Something was feeling my face with light fingers:
a moth, perhaps.
Bats were about. One touched the top of my head.
There was a wind coming up.
But there was still traffic in the distance.
I thought I could see light catching the edges of trees.
If I looked up, the stars were still there.
Where was the moon, then?
And where were the other people
who were meant to be there?

9

Everything out there is nothing to do with me:
it speaks a foreign language.
I can learn the rules but I will never speak it.
I touch the glass:
the smoothness of its surface
flatters my fingertips but,
in spite of looking,
my world is locked inside.

10

There could be music
played upon the harp in secluded valleys
or sung, in chorus, on hillsides thick with sheep.

The skylark in upward flight
has no pretensions:
he just sings.
And the moon
which touches my fingertips with silver
exercises the kind of frivolity
only the truly serious can afford.

The two philosophers
debate in the calmest of voices their own demise,
and darkness closes on their false deliberations.

The wisest end in tears
and, after the games are over,
there are other matters to while away the time.

11

A blackbird busies itself about a worm,
an elderly pigeon waddles under the rose bush,
a van goes by, slamming over the humps,
a 737 takes off for Amsterdam.
So what?

I take them as I find them.

12

Eyes that see nothing peer into my own
and look for light
where there is only darkness.
Why do you thus intrude upon my will,
suggesting things I had not thought to think
before you thought them?
You are the emptiness I cannot speak
because I have no language.
You are the presence everywhere insistent
but lacking purpose.
You are the shadows falling across the lawn
and reaching to a house
where a man sits typing,
dreaming of worldliness.
It never happens.

13

We are savaged by want,
bred in the litter of torn discarded values,
fed on the garbage dredged for our amusement
from the sewers of shame and deceit.

Beware when,
at last,
usurping the cruel whore who holds the purse-strings,
we even the score.

14

Like an old fisherman
the etymologist drags his heavy trawl
as an old gardener drags his clogging rake,
heaping the swollen falls of autumn
after the fat of summer.

15

Hearing the beetles
beating against the windows of this lighted room
is to be reminded of dispossession:
instincts which compel but are not owned,
compulsions which are part of our own natures,
defining as they destroy,
greater than any aspirations we might have,
than any desire for another kind of order.

They are just what they are:
where they are from
is where they drive us: we, the dispossessed
of rights to the very territory which is us.

The outside that we learn
is us within,
the only perfect marriage,
and what we learn we lose by learning it.

Who dares protest against his origins
when every protest is a part of them?

So, as these beetles learn the obdurate glass
they learn themselves by doing what they do
and all they learn is lost by doing it.

Their common destiny is dispossession:
they are possessed by what they cannot own.

16

We apply our reason to the behaviour of strangeness,
ignoring the persistence of the commonplace.
So, in accumulation of detail, we find nothing
and what is close at hand we overlook.

Outside, in a windy corridor,
someone turns over the pages of an enormous picture book
looking for brighter colours.

Whose job is it to throw out the uneaten sandwiches
for the sustenance of small birds:
those scraps of reality feeding on common bread?

17

Tonight
steals from tomorrow, this year
from next.

There is an idea
of nothingness:
a vacancy so true
it dares the blood, it dares the glass
to speak.

Let it pass
into a half-smile, a mere turn
of the lip.

The fires burn.
Do you see them?
Catch a burst of flame off the crystal.

The name is *Watch*.
The time *Ever*:

slowly, relentlessly becoming *Never*.

18

And it's always like this:
the omnipresent roar
rising from that other nation
as the home-team scores
yet another goal.
And the earth shudders.
And sense is swallowed, whole.

19

In the stores,
gliding through alleys stacked with ornament
the sylphs are at their play,
splashing their gold and silver on the glass.
Their lips are lurid red and their powdered faces
white with imprisoned life.
Fingers, like claws, clutch at the coloured jewels
that spill, like fish, among the silverware.

Slender as wisps of smoke
they flow among the glitter,
dreaming of conquest.
Their forsaken lovers are trampled underfoot.

20

In the butcher's
meat is cleft in two.

The butcher, glancing briefly at the chops,
scans the sliced meats.
He wipes his bloodied hands on his apron,
cleans the tip of his nose with the back of a wrist,
then smiles openly, blazing with warmth,
as a woman enters with her shopping list.

Down comes the cleaver. Bang.
The sharpest of slim knives slips through the flesh
and pares it to the bone.

The scent of meat wafts over her flared nostrils.

21

Outside, the beggars slide lower to the pavement,
affecting the droop of dying flowers,
flaunting their poverty like abandoned Lears.

I bring the small change of a lifetime.

Their dogs, brimming with health,
fed with the best of carnage,
lie on cushions.

How many coins
tarnished with the guilt of benevolence
are pressed into dirty hands?

How are the mighty poor?

Dark, dark, dark,
they all go into the dark
and the darkness swallows them all.

22

I do not understand suffering.
I look at the image of the God of Suffering
and understand nothing.

Pain I forget before I can describe
what it's like.
Relief, fleeting, becomes remote.

I do not understand suffering.
On the faces of others only can I study
its infinite mystery, its finite horror.

23

Everything dissolves into the distance
beyond the distance
that was never really there

as the city was never really there:

just people, just people,
coming and going,
living today as though there were no tomorrow

as there never is,
when the end comes.

24

There is all time to spare
in the space of nowhere
where nothing happens:
where he might be
perhaps
a tree
or its shadow, leaning to one side
in a light breeze.

Somewhere a knife explores his disease.

He will be here again,
and when he comes-to
the view outside the window
he looks through
will be there,

oblivious to the stare of one who,
as shadows pass,
as trees move in the wind,
is leaves, is grass.

25

Where are the mountains I scaled
and the roar of the falls?
Where is the dust I blew from my palms?
And where are the trees that bent in the wind
as I rounded the last corner?
See the valley as it spreads before me
with its thread of migrating cattle
and the odd, solitary, windmill.

I tighten laces
and prepare to descend the rock face.
The wind howls around me
as I feel for the next crack
in which to wedge a toe.
My fingers are white
as I hang on to life.

And there it stretches:
way down below me
winding its way towards a lost horizon.

26

Shore leave:
the ferry bar
below decks
crammed with matelots:
thirsty, savage, noisy.

They rise and sway with the boat,
pints in hand,
and survey the sea through the scuttles then, slowly,
sink, sink, sink
into the depths
with fish, with mud, the odd patrolling crab
and, finally,
rest.

The tide goes out and washes them away.

27

The knot tight,
lugged at by a lively breeze,
and the mind
spirited as the lifted sail
catches happily in the wind.

The easy heel of the boat
holding her way,
the tiller firm to the wrist.
Steady as she goes,
riding the tide, wind-kissed.

Play of ideas,
notions, a change of course,
perhaps more.
Play of wave against rock,
sea against shore
and always the knot holding
as before.

28

The stubble fields stream by
with the odd, rocking, slightly unstable
farm
and the flash of a crossing.

This is a rickety world
and don't forget it.

29

I am alone now, far from things that flatter,
listening ears, as new dramas shatter
a world of noise.

There is a busyness, a to-and-fro
outside me, where the hurried go
about a harassed world caught
in the here and now.

The battles I fought
are yesterdays that fill the world with fact
until the final fiction, the last fathomless act.

A fine despair
haunts the randomly poisoned air.

30

I sit on an easy chair
looking out across the grounds
to the river.
Around me, students (mostly Arabs)
gather into large groups,
smoke and shout at each other.
I hear odd words and phrases
of the Arabic I once spoke:
a mental phrasebook
littered with incidentals.

You could walk through the noisy, bustling *souk*
and through the claustrophobic, drowsy streets,
further and further:
shadows in doorways, the lame dog,
the donkey against the wall,
the bleating panic of a herd of goats.
The black-robed women
slid past your outer vision
in a swathe of dust and pots,
and water from the well.
And further on, the sun beat on your head
like the hammer of God,
demanding you be still.

As still, at last, I am,
looking at green lawns
down to a fresh river which flows
with all the water an Arab could ever want.

31

And so I look outside to find myself:
the garden looks the same as it did then.
The trees bud forth, the flowers search the light,
the bird that sang opens its beak to sing.
I cannot hear him.

I who, in my youth, could almost hear a pin drop
can now barely hear the doorbell ring.
One who, in youth, had curly thick brown hair
sees in the mirror a white-haired adolescent
frightened of shadows.

Who is this person who blinks and turns away?

32

Slowly, the loose coals shrink
from red to a flickering star,
a spark of life,
a blink of hope.

But never a sign of anything more than this.

What is a dying fire?
Be honest.
Resign your fantasies.

Know
that passion was young and rash,
that everything must go,
that flame must turn to ash,
that fire would have it so.

33

It's still dark.
I think I can think
as I lie here
thinking:

thinking about train times
seed packets
a button off a jacket
plums.

I can see the wardrobe
and
if I close my eyes
millions of stars

disappearing
as I stare
into the vast darkness of my head.

Who am I?
Is the itch under my right shoulder
me?

I travel down the outside
of my left leg
and sense a lost foot
its instep dead on the sheet.

Are you there?

34

The city is frayed,
nibbled by fear.
Underpasses are sprayed at night. Near
and silent, death
spreads like a stain.
There's not a breath of wind.
It begins to rain:
insistent, after dark,
it comes in a broad sweep
across the empty park.
The gutters weep.
Water butts lean
in sorrowful heaviness.

All is governed tonight
by the gathering sound of the head-shaved,
tattooed tribes who fight
at the other end of the city, in the football ground,
gathering in mobs to jeer.
They sway in delirium.
Lost in a sea of beer.

The street walls pass them by
enriched with signatures.
There are clouds of purest white
up there above the stadium roof,
while below
under a great canopy of shadow
the beasts roar:
such magnificent emphasis!

such packed enthusiasm!
These are the anthems
that bring their hearts to war.

The pavement is littered with fag-ends
and patched with blackened gum.
They are in a world of plastic bags and dog-shit.
The hole at their feet is filling up with sand.

Where will they go when the world empties?
When the song stops
and the scarves are dipped in blood?

35

I'm afraid of those memories:
I fear them, fear them utterly:
my own misshapen pasts come to alarm me.
Death after death was what their cause demanded
and I was foully compromised at last.

It wasn't me who caught them: others spoke
more eloquently than me.
I only played a small part in that drama:
was mostly in the wings,
hovering near make-up, tampering with props.
The lighting, to me, was one more mystery.

I didn't want the part I had to play,
but never once refused it:
coward to the last.

36

The days are shorter now
and nothing feeds
the pleasantries we spoke in younger days:
sunlight long gone.

The shades are longer, too,
and less defined,
as if they searched the dimness for a form
lost in ambiguities.

37

If you cared to hear,
you might, by concentration,
sense the snow gathering in distant hills.

It will sweep the northern fells
in a cloak of whiteness
which stretches from edge to edge
of the hidden landscape,

so that the children,
emerging from a world of electric light,
will be surprised by its brightness
and dazzled by its fallen stars.

38

Or see this:
it's one of my ancestors made up from fossils
and built to dominate.
See how it towers over the arctic fox.

Those who wander softly among the exhibits
peering at butterflies or pictures of ants
hardly seem alarmed.
A small boy touches a shin and is told off.
His tiny finger-prints are on the metal.

Ancestor, if you spoke, would you tell the story
of bogs and heaths and newts in miry ponds
and ever-changing weather, like it is now,
sunny one minute then cloudy the next?

Of course not.
You lumbered across the landscape looking for food
but never said a thing.
Your vocal cords, assuming of course you had them,
were tuned to other matters:
a mating call, perhaps, or roar of anger
at finding your favourite supper filched by migrants.

The exotic butterfly, next to the ants, on the right,
is somehow related to your heavy presence
by patterns of genes so complex the actual story
is lost in the plot.
Those who unravel it, dazzled by its meaning,

look on you, monster, and butterflies like this,
as wonderful icons of a rich, unfolding drama.

I only wait, here by the lonely musk ox, the great auk,
looking at things which, beautiful or ugly,
are still and dead

as I will be one day.

39

An ornithological commonplace
hoots over a demographic region, urban.
A bit of entomology runs across the carpet.
Politics has shut its mouth for once.
Philosophy climbs the stairs.

A biological specimen undresses,
moves through forty-five degrees into bed.
Theology prays.
The machine unwinds.

Hostilities cease forthwith.

40

As torchlight
opens up hidden corners

or candle flame
throws its twisted head
towards shadows

as night is rinsed of dark
and loosened light
spreads its presence
over gathered rooftops

as meaning slowly lightens
into sense.

41

Having spent much of his life
wondering what it was all about,
he sat, now old, before the dying fire
(head cradled in hands)
watching the coals turn grey
and feeling the draught at his back.
Another Christmas was over.

On the tea-stained tray at his feet
lay one remaining hazel nut.
Bending (short of breath, rheumatic)
he picked it up in his stiff fingers
and cracked it, with difficulty,
between his false teeth.

Spitting out the fragments of useless shell,
he ate it
and felt bad.

42

He's asleep.
Today's newspaper lies, unread, on his lap
and the TV shouts.
But he doesn't hear.

Where is he now?
Where will he be
when what's left of him wakes up?

I hover at the end of his bed
reluctant to wake him
even if I could.
Damaged beyond repair,
his brain journeys steadily through space
while the engine of his body
makes and remakes itself.
His paralysed arm hangs over the edge of the bed
and the future has slipped from his dead fingers.

In his abandoned study
his books line the walls.
He will never read them again.
His notes and agitated scrawls are useless now,
his files closed,
his computer switched off.
The blank screen on his monitor will never,
even briefly,
flicker into life.

Covered in dust, his pen lies
under the empty desk.
The curtain blows, listlessly,
by the open window.

Nothing remembers him
or where he came from.
Nothing knows
where he has gone.

43

Abraham has been chosen
and everything gradually
begins to move.

As the light gathers at the window
they wait for God to speak.

They huddle there
rain lashing outside
world up to its knees
in mud.

Them:
all who crowd into that little space
for comfort.

Have mercy upon them:
the memory of their sins being intolerable
and without exaggeration.

44

But now
the family grows steadily
until they are all here

chattering, drinking, eating.

I move among them
filled with the joy that is family
but can never be spoken:

all the faces I love,
that grow around me like flowers
and are gathered in:
crowded on settees,
perched on chairs,
or hovering in odd corners,
half in the light, half in the shade.

Such laughter.
Such an exchange of bounty.
Such kisses and, closer than close,
the truest of embraces.

And such departure.

45

Is it you:
sharp-sighted like a bird,
your small white face pressed against the window,
fearful of imaginary truth?

Are you peering at the curiousness of time:
its frozen moments,
the clothing of its magic

or is something out there
far too cold to touch?

46

They are speakers.
They come and go like clouds
crossing the evening sky.
There is no more to them than whispers,
if you dare.
No more than curtains drawn against the night.

47

We wake up.
The room is hard and well-defined.
Corners are neatly right-angled.
The ceiling is exactly in the right place.
The window is firmly closed against the cold.

We have an alarm clock each:
one on each side.
Both were set.
Neither went off.

Why are we awake then?
Or are we dreaming?

48

And the strangeness of it
hanging from the trees
and scattered over the rooftops.

Why are you crying?

49

Sit with him there and rest.
He never could tell you what was in his heart.

He loves you.

Yes, they are only words,
but words were his true medium:
they were as true to him as he to them.
They are the signature which ends the page.

50

He stares out at the rain
and sees it fall so gently.
Is it you, whispering in his ear?

Out in the garden, the wind lifts his hair.
Is it your hand soothes his troubled head?

Turning,
he looks behind him at the window:
he is still there,
tapping on the keys as if for ever.

There let him stay.
For the moment, time has gone out,
locking the door behind him.
Let him stay.

51

You are awash with broken blooms
bent from the stems
and risen like a flame,
twisting and rinsing, shaping
from fire to fire
a ballet of display.

Such cleansing passion
swilled and pulsed with water
drenched in fine after-thoughts of shape.
Tub after tub slides to its natural place

as you step back
and study what you have chosen.

Behind you, the massive lime is thickened with its leaves:
a thick green curtain
shaped against the sky.

And the slender birch,
like a naked body free to stretch its arms,
shakes its young tassels.

Its younger sister
shy, diminutive,
shivers with delight.

The rowan, somewhat stand-offish,
makes no show.

But the wrinkled elder
crammed against your pot-laden shed
grows and grows,
its ancient right of place
established by the accidents of nature.

52

I close my eyes.
In the profound darkness of existence
light swirls, as mysterious as the wind
which moves the clouds.
Coming from nowhere
and losing itself in distances my mind can't reach.

The appalling goodness of love covers me like a blanket.
Stars shine in my head.
I imagine the moon:
her impossible loveliness,
her miraculous quiescence.

You turn
and I touch the very heart of things with amazing
tenderness.
The incorruptibility of truth shoots through my body:
the tongue of flame that anchors me to you.

53

I remember it all:
my shed in the left bottom corner,
yours in the right.
Your greenhouse under the old apple tree.
The Himalyan Musk rose
striving through the branches towards the light.

Your bird-feeder stood proud in the grass
fronting the middle distance:
it had its own congregations.
The silver birch near the greenhouse,
more than thirty feet tall,
towered over the smaller silver birch and the rowan:
they stood motionless before the back wall.

But the trees are bare now.
Your pots are empty or stowed away.
I've gathered the fallen leaves.
The ground is damp.
The sky is heavy, grey.

How much did summer cost?
How many times did you hover over pots
in a riot of colour, feeling between the leaves?
How the heart ponders it all.
How the heart grieves.

54

We are like children
arguing over sweets
but knowing where they come from.
We dare our love by throwing stones at it
and never crying.

We probe, and poke, and pry into its secret
but never find the answer in ourselves.

55

When I look back
the distance I've covered
is lost among the foliage.

I'm nearly at the end now:
the gate will soon be closed.
There's only one way out of the garden.

It's beautiful at this time of year,
especially on a day like this:
sunshine, warmth, everything in flower.

But it's late afternoon.
Soon it will be evening.
Soon the gate will close.

For the others, it will open first thing.
It looks like being another nice day, too.

For some, tonight, it will close.
For ever.

56

I was there.
I saw it all unfold.

And all the noise was more than I could bear.

57

I looked
but it was hidden from me.

I searched the pages
but found nothing I didn't know.

I wandered among the crowds of shoppers
seeking a meaning,
but none ever came.

I thought the world looked different
but it was the same, the same.

58

It could have been so different.
There is no truer metaphor for love.